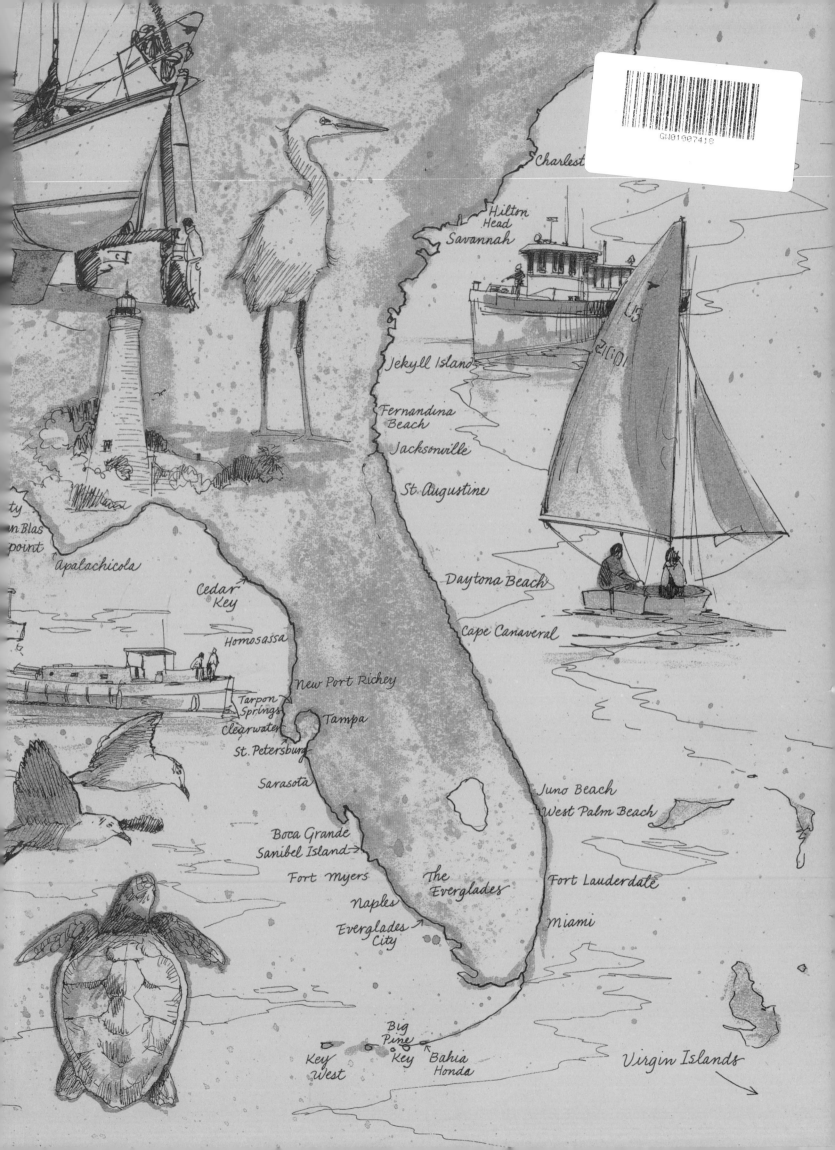

Charlest[on]

Hilton
Head

Savannah

Jekyll Island

Fernandina
Beach

Jacksonville

St. Augustine

Daytona Beach

Cape Canaveral

Apalachicola

Cedar
Key

Homosassa

New Port Richey

Tarpon
Springs

Clearwater

Tampa

St. Petersburg

Sarasota

Juno Beach

West Palm Beach

Boca Grande

Sanibel Island

Fort Myers

The
Everglades

Fort Lauderdale

Naples

Miami

Everglades
City

Big
Pine
Key

Bahia
Honda

Key
West

Virgin Islands

August '93.

A wonderful holiday —
in the Gulf of Mexico —
these pictures serve to remind us of
St. Pete's → Naples — and Captiva!

SOUTHERN SHORES

Copyright © 1989
Sentinel Communications Company
633 N. Orange Avenue
Orlando, Florida 32801

Illustrated and written by Roger Bansemer
Edited by Dixie Kasper
Calligraphy by Linda Renc
Jacket and titles designed by Katie Pelisek
Printed in Hong Kong by South Sea International Press Ltd.
First Edition 1989.

Library of Congress Cataloging-in-Publication Data
Bansemer, Roger.
    Southern Shores / by Roger Bansemer.
        p.   cm.
    "Sentinel books"
    ISBN 0-941263-08-8 : $35.95
    1. Florida — Description and travel — 1981. 2. Coasts
    — Florida. 3. Natural history — Florida. 4. Florida in art.
    5. Coasts in art. 6. Bansemer, Roger — Journeys —
    Florida. I. Title.
    F316.2.B27 1989
    917.5904'63'09146 — dc20   89-33767
                                                    CIP

SOUTHERN SHORES

Roger Bansemer

Roger Bansemer paints the wonders of nature in his three-story studio in the woods near a meandering creek. It is here that he commits tender memories to canvas. Often his macaws, Neon and Taco, perch nearby. And now and then a wild bird wanders in the studio's open door to retrieve spilled seeds.

The Clearwater, Florida, artist is versatile, equally at ease with finely detailed etchings and hundred-foot-tall murals. Malcolm Forbes called Bansemer's first book, *The Art of Hot-Air Ballooning,* the most beautiful, colorful, imaginative, artful depiction of the sport he had ever seen.

That first effort at putting words to paintings has helped Bansemer's career soar to new heights. Perhaps it is because he paints what he is most familiar with; his touch is sensitive and the narrative, like his paintings, is heartfelt.

Bansemer's artistry extends to the sprawling home he designed for himself in a secluded, natural setting of oaks and palmettos. It serves as the artist's perfect repose from a too-hurried world.

For my girls,
Lauren
and
Rachael

Who can resist climbing on cool river rocks worn smooth by time and polished through the ages by the running water of a mountain stream? What is the attraction they hold? Perhaps it's just some basic instinct from our past that draws us to them. In any case, water and things associated with it fascinates us.

All this water eventually runs to the sea, so what better place to start than the tributaries that feed that rich array of images along our Southern shores.

Even in a lifetime I couldn't begin to paint all the interesting sights there are relating to the water, so I've simply tried to capture what has interested me the most, knowing I'd leave much of it behind.

Hopefully places of character and beauty will always be here. For certain, many of them are quickly slipping away. While I can, I want to explore some of these places.

My first job is to get a boat to do all this exploring I'm planning. I decide on a 12-foot aluminum boat and an 8-horsepower engine. It's so light I don't even need a boat ramp to launch it. I simply pull over to the side of the road, push the craft off the trailer and easily slide my indestructible little work boat into the water. It's ideal because it's simple and in shallow water it's PERFECT.

Years ago my dad and I would canoe on Florida rivers. It was not as fashionable then to have a home on the water, so the waterways were very much untouched. Very beautiful on warm summer days.

There was always a rope swing somewhere along the way where the locals would collect. It was easy to tell when you were coming upon such a place. As bodies plunged into cold water, the shrieks and cries echoed for some distance.

An old tree – blown over by a tropical storm perhaps –
never gave up and continued to thrive despite obvious difficulties. It amazes me
how fragile the land is, yet in other ways so tough and adaptable.
It made a good spot for my Dad and me to spread out a blanket
and have lunch.

I revisited those places where as a child my family and I spent a vacation. It was on the Homosassa River, and to my surprise the trailer we stayed in was still there. It had long been forgotten, and was now nothing more than a ghost of what it had been.

One thing had not changed, and that was the giant grasshoppers about 3 inches long that still inhabited the surroundings in abundance. I won't tell you what terrible things I used to do to those poor creatures.

On hot summer days, Cicadas still carry on
their songs of raucous buzzing high in the trees.

Small rivers in the South have a slow moving
and unkempt atmosphere about them. Some of it
becomes part of the natural beauty of weathering—
like the fish house. Other elements, like the tires,
just unattractively hang on, reminding us that some
things never seem to fit in even if they do serve a purpose.

One of the joys of floating down a river is finding some unexpected beauty around the next bend. Something that just grew there on its own without the benefit of human hands. If I tried to make these grow I probably would have lousy luck with them, but nature has an amazing way of taking care of itself when left alone. The yard around my studio is sort of like that, and I always delight in discovering wildflowers that have popped up from nowhere. I think there's too much fuss over keeping one's property manicured with just the right hedges and bushes, mowing, fertilizing and all that. Nature has always had a beautiful way of expressing itself without man's help.

On the other hand, some plants
get carried away with themselves
and do cause problems.
The water hyacinth was introduced
into this country from South America.
As beautiful as they are, they quickly
clog up lakes and rivers
and make waterways impassible.
Their roots use up all the oxygen
in the water and also block out
available sunlight. Not a great plant
to have growing in your pond – especially
if you're a fish. On the bright side,
they do a good job helping clean up
streams man has carelessly polluted
by absorbing sewage and industrial wastes
from the water. They may also be used
as cattle feed.

The most amazing thing about the
water hyacinth is that its growth doubles
every 10 days.

Ducks seem to make themselves at home anywhere, but it's always
a delight to come across a clutch of baby Muscovies following their mom.
You would think they would all look the same, yet they each
have their own individual markings and personality.
Not much different than the family of man.

I'm going to get into all the birds that are so typical of Southern shores later, but I couldn't resist painting these personable creatures.

The white ones are Pekin ducks. They originally came from China. The other one is a female mallard. The male mallard is one of the most beautiful and well-known ducks in the world. His colors are magnificent.

They all look like high-speed vacuum cleaners when they're eating, and pet names usually end up being either Hoover or Kirby.

River banks and out-of-the-
way inlets are favorite places
to abandon old cars, but time
absorbs them into the landscape
and, in a strange sort of
way, they too take on a
character that
fascinates me.

Once these cars stood on a showroom floor. New owners washed and
polished them, and the slightest dent or scratch
would be of big concern.
It's interesting to think about.

The cabbage palm offers
a convenient spot for
turtles to sun themselves.

Here, wildflowers
cast soft images
on the water.
A sharp contrast
to what man has left behind.

This ferry has been operating out of Salt Springs, Florida, since 1910, crossing the St. Johns River.

In this "rush-around" society, it is nice to see a service like this still operating. I sometimes feel it would be an ideal job, although in reality I'm sure I would get bored with it quickly.

The method for reversing direction intrigues me. A simple trailer hitch allows the tender to pivot around. It's good when someone figures out simple yet effective ways of doing things. I like that. You know if this were made by some large corporation it would be full of gears, pulleys and motors and probably wouldn't work near as well as this homemade affair.

Near Jacksonville I put my boat on another ferry boat to cross the St. John's River. It's a crazy world.

Almost gone are the little general stores
that carry everything you could ever need.
What K mart doesn't have can probably be found
on the shelves of these little places.
At least it seems that way.

I drove up to one such place
called Treasure Camp on the
Suwanee River.

I couldn't resist doing this portrait
of Edmund and his dog Eddie.
Their eyebrows fascinated me.

When was the last time you walked into a 7 Eleven and had them offer you a free cup of coffee just to be friendly?

Alice, the owner, (that was her dad, Edmund) shared stories along with the coffee about a treasure worth millions that was buried by a pirate, maybe Jean Lafitte, in the river just outside the store. During the '20s someone tried digging it up with dredging equipment, and supposedly brought up one chest.

Then the project failed as sand and silt collapsed into the shaft where the treasure was buried. Since then, I would imagine there have been more stories than treasure, but who knows.

The last floating bridge in Florida, called the Overstreet Bridge
and located near Mexico Beach, had its
days numbered as I sketched it.
Another disappearing relic of the waterways
making way for the new.

On the other side of the bridge was another
charming relic, Patrick's Store.

All this was being dwarfed and pushed aside
by a new bridge being built, and all the
lives and history which centered around
this place for so many years will
now be passed over at 65 m.p.h.

I felt like a time traveler as I looked at this place that at one time was a hub of activity. This was the classic general store with bolts of cloth, flour and rice. Now it had made way for candy bars and motor oil. Yet the charm was still there, right down to the old scales and the small post office window still in operation for the locals who saunter in.

The lady who operated the store had been there
since 1940 and took it over from her father, Patrick,
who built it in 1916.

My sense of being in the past was quickly
disrupted when I purchased a postcard as a
remembrance and was told, "That will be a dollar
and a half." So much for the past.

Here is one item that is definitely out of the past - the motor court. There are a few remaining, but generally they are abandoned or in disrepair.

I like the idea of parking right in front of the room. It was easy to unload all the paraphernalia you took with you on a trip, and staying in a little house made you feel like you were staying in, well, a little house, instead of those large hotels where you have to lug your bags through impersonal, interior-decorated lobbies, wait in line at some check-in counter and then have to walk half a mile down those dreadful hallways, knowing every room is the same except for the number on the door.

Although the motor courts always seemed to have that peculiar smell about them, I like it better than being kenneled up in those bastilles that look like a computer-generated tower of Legos. Besides, the peculiar smell always seemed to disappear after about a half-hour.

There are many interesting structures along the coast. I can appreciate the homemade ones, at least they have some character.

Then there are the restaurants and such, designed by professionals, which can look insufferably bad. I couldn't believe my eyes when I came across this one. Incredible!

No less attractive are Navy ships. They're clothed with layer upon layer upon layer of gray pigment. Believe me, I know. I served on this carrier. I hated it, but I'll have to admit it was exciting to see those jets take off and land on the pitching deck. I used to sneak way up on the structure above the stack, and look down on them landing.

I'm not sure why I'm including them here. Maybe it has something to do with what America is all about. This certainly is a wondrous place, and these ships help give us the opportunity to create things like the restaurants on the preceding page, strange as they are. I'm all for it.

VF-41

804

VF-41   5746

NAVY

Lots of interesting buildings along the coast to paint.

This house at Seaside above Panama City is built new to look old. ↑

This house near St. Augustine
was built to look like a lighthouse.

What a nice place to work and watch the world go by, I thought, until I
realized all the diesel truck fumes that must get pumped up there.

It's amazing the variety of lifestyles people have. In Miami, Vizcaya stands as a monument to one man's achievement. Nearby I found these houseboats which stand for a completely different set of values. It's hard to know who's really better off in the long run. I guess for me somewhere between the mansion and the houseboat would be just fine.

Being content with one's self can lie within any kind of shelter called home.

It may be that cormorant, sitting up there with nothing in the world to be concerned about but drying his wings and catching fish, has the best lifestyle of all.

Isn't it amazing what man creates. And to think it has all been built in the last generation or so. I can't help but wonder what the Spanish explorers would think if they could see all this. I feel exceedingly insignificant with my 12-foot boat.

If you're wondering, this is a giant fender. When in place it keeps the ship from bashing itself against the side of the dock.

These props are obviously big, but they get even larger— up to 35 feet in diameter and costing more than a half-million dollars. Most of them are made of bronze, some of stainless steel.

How is this for a comparison? This is the prop from my boat.

Tugboat. What a great name. Tugboat.
   There must be something in our childhood that makes us
look upon these boats as being cute.
   A cute 4,000 horsepower tugboat and a man in a rowboat
producing about one-tenth horsepower.

If you're into heavy-duty projects, here is the ultimate handyman special.
This ship was just leaving Jacksonville on its way to the
Caribbean with a cargo of propane. It appears someone
may not have been observing the no-smoking sign.
The deck reminded me of one of those aluminum pop-top
cans with peanuts or some other thing inside. It's
sometimes a struggle to get those flimsy lids off.
Can you imagine the force it took to open up this deck?
When I inquired about it I was told it was not
that unusual an occurrence to have a propane explosion
aboard ship. Really makes you want to travel the
world on one of these freighters!

If that repair project appears to be
a little too much for you to tackle,
this fishing boat may be more what
you're looking for. Barnacles
may be what's holding this one together
and, for certain, a few
well-placed chisel strokes
on this prop would
be in order
for a
smoother ride.

Artistically, boats out of water are much more pleasing to paint. I love to see the graceful sweep of the hull followed through to its conclusion, rather than broken up by water and waves.

The sailboat on the next page is my favorite. I found it rotting away near Jacksonville. It's just another 20th century discard, but it has this great prehistoric look about it. It was certainly a fine yacht in its day; now only dry bones remain. This one would also make a great project on the weekends ... but not for me.

What I don't like about boats is that they require constant attention, especially wooden-hulled boats, or they end up like this. I would much rather do paintings of them than own them.

This lifeboat once graced the elegant decks of the Queen Mary. Now she belongs to a young sign painter. He dreams of restoring the rusted shell to original condition. Maybe he will, but for now the main concern is to fix the gaping hole his small wooden dinghy punched in the side of this once-hefty steel-hulled vessel during a storm. Not a good indication of its seaworthiness. But sometimes impossible dreams die hard when you're young. From what he told me about not having any money, I do not share his optimism for the project although I do share his hopes. He was patching that hole, temporarily needless to say, with duct tape to keep out water from the wake of passing boats. I wished him the best as I left.

I often wonder what has become of that nostalgic vessel.

For years, Saint Michael's Church in Charleston has been a gathering place for ladies who make and sell wreaths, dried flowers and handsome sweet-grass baskets.

Two centuries ago, Belgium blocks were brought over in sailing ships as ballast and then used to make streets.
These indestructible old stones were being relaid in a restored part of town.
What a job!

It's hard to pick one or two images
to express a feeling about a whole city.
Charleston has about 2,000 beautifully
restored buildings and each one
has its own unique story.

Saint Philips Church, with its
interesting old cemetery, makes a
nice place to sit and reflect
under century-old trees.

Horse-drawn carriages filled with
tourists slowly make their way
through the city, drivers pointing
out bits of history as they go.
I've never taken one of these
carriages, but it really looks
pleasant. I'm going to do it
next time I'm here.

Savannah is another one of those cities where there is so much history, it becomes a bit overwhelming, but what fascinates me the most is the incredible variety of textures on the buildings.

Most of these buildings on the waterfront were once used as warehouses for cotton. Now they have become interesting little shops and restaurants.

This is a statue of Florence Martus, better known as the waving girl. For 44 years from 1887 to 1931, no ship arrived or departed day or night without greetings from Florence waving her hand or a lantern. She lived on nearby Elba Island. Not many people met her, yet she became a legend in ports around the world.

Just to the east of Savannah
I found this lighthouse
on Tybee Island. I have
always liked little add-on buildings
and out-buildings.
The proportions of these seemed
especially nice.
I think I'll make a point
to visit more lighthouses
and maybe do a section
in this book about them.

In fact, a whole book
of them would
be nice.

In Georgia, Jekyll Island was the place to be if you were a multimillionaire. The Rockefellers, Morgans and Goulds all wintered here from 1886 to 1942. Then, strangely enough, most of it was deserted. Now it has become a state park. This was their clubhouse, now a hotel on the island.

Jekyll Island Wharf
was built in 1886.

The marshland all along this area is quite beautiful.

This was the Juno Beach Pier. The Gulf Stream
came close to shore in this area, which made for good fishing
I'm told, but a hurricane took out a section of the pier.

Several months later I went back and discovered
it had been replaced with these apartments —
complete with fence and a small red "no trespassing"
sign on the gate. I wonder if we will look back
years from now on this new building and remark
how interesting it is
or what charming
character it has.
Somehow I doubt it.

The old place with its metal roof and wood siding seemed more inviting
and had a warmth that cannot be matched by concrete and plastic.
    I think architects should spend more time outside. If
they were to set up their drawing boards on location as
artists do their easels, we might see more buildings
that fit in with their surroundings.

Have you ever noticed all these condominiums are named after the things they bulldozed out of existence? Think about it. Many beach areas now are virtually inaccessible because of these places. I can't help but have a little disdain for places that appear to lock residents in and everyone else out.
The days when we all left our doors unlocked are pretty much gone forever, I know, but this guardhouse is a little too much.

The one good thing about condominiums is that they put a lot of people in a relatively small space, but they're not for me. I only wish they would put them further back from the beach and give other people a chance to enjoy what should be for everyone.

I guess it's nice if you live there, and something to complain about if you don't. It's just that I wonder when it will all end. When will there be enough buildings right on the water? Every one of these has sprung up since I was a boy, and I have a feeling it won't stop until all our shorelines look like New York City in a leisure suit.

St. Augustine, the nation's oldest city, has managed somehow to maintain its sense of charm, and the history here is preserved in such a way as to make it fun. That's what makes this town one of my favorite places.

The fort at St. Augustine, Castillo de San Marcos, is more than 300 years old and built entirely of coquina shell stone, which I understand is a lost art.

Here a friendly park ranger tells children all about the fort.

If you happened to be a foot soldier when this fort was in service, you would have earned $75... a year.

If you had been a gunner in charge of a cannon like this, you would have made $112 a year. A ration allowance of 53 cents a day came with that.

Unfortunately, deductions for issues of food, uniforms, weapons repair, medical and the expected charitable contributions usually exceeded the actual pay. Some things never change.

A nice way to see the city is by taking one of these horse-drawn carriages.

There is so much here that I can't begin to list all there is to see,
but I do know that exploring the streets is as enjoyable now
as when I was a small boy on vacation with my parents.

This house, the Fernandez-Llambias House,
was built sometime before 1763, during the
first Spanish colonial period.

In St. Augustine you can see the oldest wooden schoolhouse, built more than 200 years ago while Florida was still under Spanish rule. It was put together with wooden pegs and hand-made nails.

This is the oldest house in St. Augustine, built shortly after the British burned the city to the ground in 1702.

All these fascinating historical places are interspersed with more fun things to see, like this one-man band.

The Lightner Museum is one of my favorites. It was originally built by millionaire Henry Flagler as a hotel. Now it houses a variety of curiosities and antiques including art, furniture, Art Nouveau, and some incredible glass pieces.

These are the Old City Gates of St. Augustine. I like their simple statement of strength.

A huge lion at the head of this bridge
acknowledges my departure as I head south.

Miles of beautiful beaches still exist from St. Augustine to Daytona.

Daytona Beach
is one of the few places
where you can drive a car
on the beach, but an
early-morning bicycle ride
seems more appropriate.

There are several places with that carnival boardwalk atmosphere that everyone says they like to stay away from, yet ends up going to. Daytona is one, Panama City near the Panhandle is another. Years ago I spent my summer there spraying names and beach scenes on T-shirts with an airbrush. I rode this roller coaster then.

When I painted this, the roller coaster had fallen into disrepair and was no longer in use. Made me feel kind of old.

Myrtle Beach in South Carolina is another fun town, but the last time I was there it did nothing but rain.

At Cape Canaveral, just south
of Daytona Beach, is one of our
country's greatest marvels.
And the ultimate ride.

No matter where you travel along Southern shores, you are sure to find places that sell souvenirs like this.

One of my first recollections of visiting Florida is getting a miniature box of candy oranges to take home. Tacky as such things are, they're all wonderful in their own way, and if you have children, watching their eyes light up at the sight of a souvenir such as one of these shell marvels may make them worth the price.

Lamps made from conch shells
with plastic flamingos.

Heading toward the southernmost tip of
the United States you will cross the Seven Mile Bridge
at Bahia Honda. Now there are two bridges connecting the Keys.
One stands as a monument to obsolescence. Built in the late '30's, it has fallen
into disrepair. Sections have been taken out to prevent access, but many areas
have been left as great long piers for fishermen. Unlike many European cultures
ours seems to prefer replacing bridges rather than repairing them.

On my way to Key West I stopped at Big Pine Key to see the Key Deer. I found a raccoon instead, tossed him part of my sandwich and before I knew it about 20 of these aggressive bandits flocked around my van, begging for a share of what was going to be my supper. I sacrificed my peanut butter and ate at a restaurant that night.

Before it got dark, I did find what I was looking for... the Key Deer. Only 250 or 300 of these beautiful animals still exist. About as many are getting killed each year by cars and such as are being born. Loss of habitat is also a problem. They live only on Big Pine Key and a few small islands they can swim to.

It's illegal to feed the deer. I'm not sure about the raccoons. I hope they all survive. It would be a shame to lose them.

Here are a few things
that come to mind when I think
of Key West.

Ernest Hemingway wrote many books
here, including A Farewell to Arms
and For Whom the Bell Tolls.
He loved cats and shared his house with
50 or 60 of them until his death in 1961.
Now about 40 cats still reside here, all descendants of
the author's pets.

One of the tour guides told me it cost more than $600.
a month just to feed them. That seemed like a lot to me
until I figured out it came to 50¢ a day per cat.

The Conch Train has symbolized Key West for as long as I can remember.

And of course, Mel Fisher's treasure from the Spanish galleon Atocha is also on display there. Sixteen years of struggle and disappointment finally paid off for him with the largest treasure of gold and silver ever found.

As I was walking around Key West I kept my eye on a blimp flying at several thousand feet out over the open sea. The next day the ship pulled in, obviously a tether point for the helium-filled craft. Upon asking what the thing was for, I was told by a uniformed official, "We can't tell you; ask one of the townies, they all know." I forgot to ask, but my guess is it has something to do with surveillance.

Without question the foremost landmark in Key West is Sloppy Joe's Bar, Hemingway's favorite hangout.

Pink and turquoise seem an appropriate and pleasing color scheme for the Keys. The Conch houses are part of what gives Key West its charm. This massive column of unattractive concrete marks the southernmost tip of the United States, just 90 miles from Cuba.

Laid-back merchants of shells and souvenirs display their goods on makeshift tables so typical of the Key West lifestyle.

Beyond Key West lies the Caribbean,
and the further you wander into this tropical region
the more slow-motion the lifestyle becomes.
Getting from one place to another varies greatly, depending on
how much time you have and how much you have to spend.

The Norway is so large, at some ports of call it has to anchor offshore.

No matter what ship you take, when you step off that gangplank you become
fair game for the tourist industry.

In the American Virgin Islands, from St. Thomas I watched clouds build up
   in late afternoon over St. John.
St. John, much of which is preserved as a national park, has some of the most
   beautiful beaches I have ever seen.

Vivian has lived on an island, Salt Island, almost all of her life. As far as I know, only two other people live there. She raises some chickens and goats, and when sailboats stop at her beach, they sometimes leave her some food. There's no electricity.

Not many people in this world have a Robinson Crusoe type of existence, so I felt I was meeting someone quite special. When I asked this simple, loving woman what it was like, she answered me in her charming island way, "I have a battery radio, can go swimming, can go fishing, so you see, I'm obviously happy."

We talked for a long time, with the whitest sand and the bluest water I had ever seen at our feet. She shared many stories with me about her life and her island and when I left, she gave me a coconut.

I will always remember her.

The Virgin Islands support themselves
primarily by tourism.
Much of it is from the sale
of already manufactured
imported items such as
jewelry and perfume, but
occasionally you will find
someone using their own
hands to create something
of worth and beauty.

In our world of fast food
and disposable cameras,
it was nice to see this lady
sitting in the warm
tropical breeze,
probably doing what her
mother did before her,
in a patient and caring way.
Society has become too
mechanized and regimented.
Too much 9 to 5.
And in so doing, a lot
of the enjoyment is lost
and then the creativity vanishes.

But when work is performed in the spirit of service and love, it becomes worship.
I could see it in this lady's face.

A small boat like this is used to carry cargo from island to island.

My dog, Lady, hates a bath with the hose
but give her a chance to swim at the beach
and she'll be the
first one in.

Part of the fun
in getting wet is a
chance to sprawl out
in the sun afterward to dry off.

Years ago our family had an
unusual cat who actually enjoyed
the water.

I have always enjoyed painting beach people. It's one of the only social gathering places where people can dress like this, and about the only place you see people as they really are.

This is my girl, Lauren.

And this is my other girl, Rachael.
Her bathing suit is on backwards
because I didn't know the ruffle was
supposed to be in the back.

There is nothing more special than
watching them grow and discover
new things every day.
They are both very special.

Here are some interesting shapes!

We share
the beaches with
turtles like these.
The difference is they rely on beaches
for their survival. Eggs are laid in the sand,
more than 100 at a time, and incubate
in about two months.
    Raccoons eat many of the eggs; humans steal,
sell and eat them; and after they hatch, birds and
other predators get the baby turtles on their way to the water.
        Such things as lights from apartment buildings also
confuse turtles in their search for the water. Lights also
hinder nesting, and coastal construction hasn't helped.
            Fish nets also drown many turtles.

At the Children's Museum of Juno Beach,
Florida, a fiberglass patch is inspected
which was applied months earlier
on an injured green sea turtle.
The turtle was tagged and released
back into the Atlantic Ocean.

Tagged turtles have been found
as far away as New England
and even Africa.

Manatees

Only 1,200 of these curious and friendly creatures remain in our waters. The manatee's or sea-cow's worst enemy is of course, who else, man. Although extreme cold and red tide are two natural causes of death, the most common are boat propellers, loss of habitat and feeding grounds, poaching, and pollution. Fish hooks and monofilament line entanglement are also a problem. More are dying each year than are being born, and because the manatee bears young only every 3 to 5 years it is easy to see why it is on the endangered species list. These pleasant creatures grow to a length of 10 to 15 feet and weigh an average of 2,000 to 3,500 pounds. Generally slow-moving, they can reach a speed of 15 m.p.h. for short spurts. They eat an incredible 60 to 100 pounds of aquatic plants a day, helping to keep rivers clear. They also were believed to be the creatures ancient mariners mistook for mermaids. That's what being at sea too long can do.

You may see a sign like
this along many rivers
and inlets.
It pretty much
says it all.

The water temperature even in Florida can sometimes drop
below 72 degrees in the winter, which can be
life-threatening to the warm-blooded manatee.
For that reason, you will often see them
congregate by the discharge of power plants
where the water is warm. This utility company
by Tampa Bay has built a viewing dock
for the public.

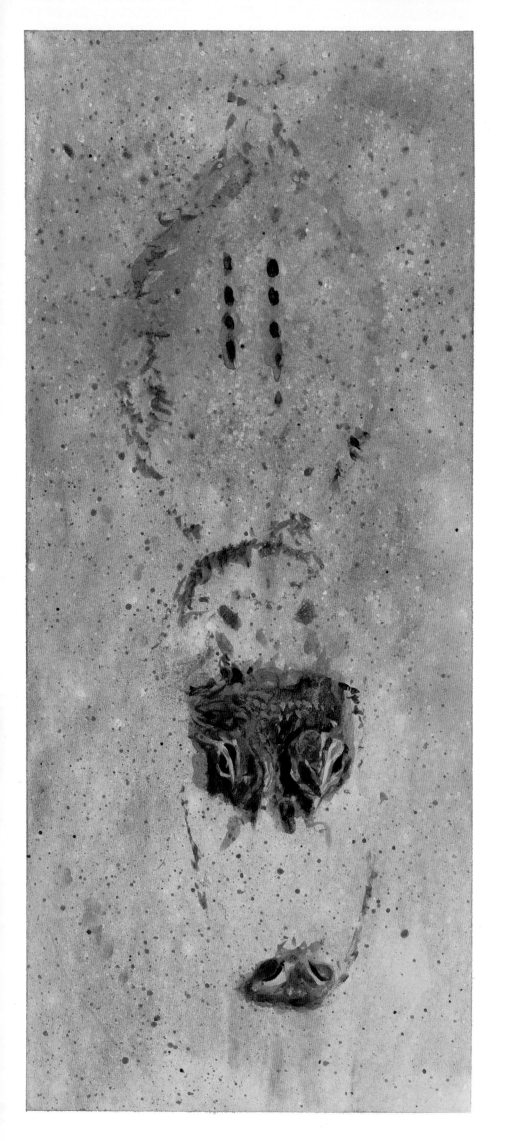

On the other end of the spectrum from the gentle manatee is one of the original citizens of Florida, the alligator, gliding through a layer of duckweed. When I was growing up we had a lake in our back yard with an alligator in it. We always figured the alligator was more afraid of us than we were of him so we swam there. But then people started feeding marshmallows to the gator, which it loved, and it became sort of tame. Then every time it saw anyone walk down to the edge of the lake, it would paddle over to greet them. Needless to say, swimming was discontinued.

Alligators grow to be about 14 feet long. The males live longer than the females, about 30 to 35 years in the wild. They can exert a pressure of 3,000 pounds per square inch when closing their jaw.

The expression these animals have is a real mix. Is it happy, angry, full, hungry? In a strange way they have a Mona Lisa look of the wild about them. It makes me wonder what they're thinking.

When I asked this guy about dragging an alligator by the tail, he told me that they're too interested in trying to get away and won't turn around. I am not, however, totally convinced. Even a little two-foot alligator can be pretty mean.

It is true that if their stomachs are rubbed while on their backs, they fall asleep.

I guess the most appropriate place to see an alligator is in the Everglades. You don't need to take one of these airboats to see them, either. Any roadside picnic site in the area will more than likely have several alligators floating around, waiting for a handout.
Illegal, by the way. Private airboats are not allowed in the national park, thank goodness, but outside the park these vehicles scar the swamplands.

Worse yet are these swamp buggies. They are strictly for people who don't care what they leave behind. Outside the park boundaries, the Everglades are criss-crossed with trails of destruction from the tracks of these awful things. It's sometimes hard to understand man's insensitivity toward the land. Fortunately, our government has had foresight enough to set aside large areas of unique natural beauty like the Everglades National Park to protect it from vehicles like this. As large as the park is, 1.4 million acres, it still only encompasses one tenth of the total area of the Everglades. Florida already has lost 50 percent of its original forests, and right now it is losing its forest wilderness at a faster rate than South America is losing its rain forest.

The Seminole Indians who live in
the Everglades have developed a
unique style of clothing called Seminole
quilting. Using a machine to sew
may seem like a break in tradition
but, in fact, Seminole quilting always
has been a machine technique.
As early as 1880, they were using
hand-cranked sewing machines
and fabric they got from traders.

Many Seminoles still live under thatched roofs
of palmettos, called Chickees, along
Tamiami Trail. They seem to live
very private lives; however,
some villages open themselves up
for tourists to take a look.

I have no idea how
they cope with mosquitoes.

Some of the cypress trees in the Everglades were there 100 years before Columbus arrived in the New World.

This must qualify as one of the South's smallest post offices. It's in the Everglades at Ochopee on the Tamiami Trail. →

All in all, this is what you see the most of while traveling through the 'Glades. ↘

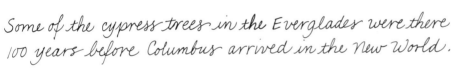

Mangroves

One of the most valuable natural resources along the southern half of Florida and the islands is the mangrove. They help prevent erosion and stabilize shorelines. They filter the water and help it stay clear. The mangroves also play an important part in providing nursery areas for all kinds of fish, shellfish and crustaceans, so when mangroves are disturbed or destroyed, ocean fish and fishing are directly affected.

Three types of mangrover grow in the South. The red mangrove grows out into the water, the black mangrove usually grows along the water's edge, and the white mangrove grows above the waterline. The red mangrove is sometimes called the "walking tree" for obvious reasons.

Mangroves grow well in salt water because they have an unusual ability to get fresh water from salt water. The red mangrove blocks salt absorption through its roots. The black mangrove secretes salt through its leaves.

The red mangrove grows these seedlings
on its branches. The bottom part of it
is heavier so when they drop off
they stick in the mud and root to grow
a new plant. Or they float away eventually
to root somewhere else.

As a boy I would find them floating
in the Gulf of Mexico while swimming.
I always called them sea-pencils and used them
to draw pictures in the waves.

This is what it looks like when they take root.
A pretty remarkable plant.

This is the black mangrove. It doesn't
have legs like the red mangrove but it has
these fingerlike projections that come up in
great numbers from the tree's roots and
provide oxygen to the plant.

Mangroves are protected and it is
unlawful to cut or prune them even on
private land without a permit.

Another very important purpose
not to be overlooked is
the nesting places the mangroves
provide for the rich assortment
of birds the South is
so fortunate to have.

Dedicated to the rescue, repair, recuperation and hopefully the release of wild birds, the Suncoast Seabird Sanctuary at Indian Shores on the west coast of Florida is the largest wild bird hospital in the United States. An incredible 6,000 injured birds are brought into the sanctuary every year.

Founder Ralph Heath told me about 90 percent of all the birds brought in have injuries or illnesses directly or indirectly related to man. He said many people wondered about the value of keeping crippled birds alive and taking care of them at the sanctuary until 1975, when two permanently crippled pelicans fledged the first baby brown pelican ever raised in captivity. Since then, more than 500 young pelicans have hatched and flown from the sanctuary.

Birds are unique indicators of our environmental quality. What affects them can potentially affect us and unfortunately, an increasing number of birds are being affected by pollution.

The white pelican is a tourist here in the South during the winter months.

With an 8-foot wingspan, they migrate from lakes in the Midwest.

The strange-looking growth on their bills occurs during the mating season.

Unlike the brown pelicans, who make spectacular dives for fish, white pelicans work together in groups, forming semi-circles and herding fish to shore where they simply scoop them up.

These two chicks are about
five weeks old. They
will be ready to leave
the nest and fly in
about three weeks.
The adult is sporting
its summer plumage,
white head and dark brown
stripe down its neck.

The pelican, like the
alligator, has a definite
prehistoric look
about it.

This is winter plumage.
Yellow head and white neck.

Every pelican has a definite
personality.
They are, by far, the most playful
and fun-loving bird I know.

They will do almost anything
for a fish.

This pelican with its summer plumage sits on its nest. Its wing is broken. Hence the odd-looking configuration of feathers. Many pelicans are injured each year from getting tangled in fishing lines.

This pelican has on its winter plumage and sits among a red mangrove. Pelicans are very intelligent birds, but like cats, they tend not to show it. I would be happy to paint a few dozen more of these great characters, but I'll do just one more.

Gulls have to be the most common bird around the water. They can materialize out of nowhere by the hundreds as quick as you can open a picnic basket. Did you know that technically there is no such bird as a sea gull? Some dictionaries don't even include the word. They are simply gulls.

This is one of the larger gulls. It's a herring gull exhibiting a characteristic shriek.

All gulls have white on them.
The exception is the immature gull.
They are brown. The laughing gull is
very common and, like the brown pelican,
it changes plumage. In the summer,
its head will become a rich black.

The great blue heron is one of our most majestic waterbirds. They are extremely territorial and even vicious toward intruding birds, to the point of sometimes killing them. In fact, they don't seem to like any birds at all, including their own kind. I guess at some point they must be friendly to each other, but rarely will you see two herons in the same area.

If a heron has a choice between eating a fish and a mouse, it will eat the mouse first. They also like frogs, snakes and other small birds.

The yellow-crowned night heron works the second shift, feeding primarily at night and thus avoiding any territorial disputes with other birds that might occur during the day. They are common sights to anyone who has spent much time along Southern shores.

They love to eat fiddler crabs and other crustaceans.

The immature night heron is not very elegant compared with the adult, which has beautiful markings.
Most shorebirds are indistinguishable as to male or female.

The black-crowned night heron
is a gorgeous little bird
but not often seen.
Below is the
yellow-crested night
heron with its white
facial markings and
beautiful bright eyes.

I have seen the tri-colored heron
nesting on powder-blue eggs
in tourist areas where
hundreds of
people walk
within a
few feet of the nests
every day. Although they
are quite similar, you can
tell them apart from the little
blue heron because they have
white feathers under their neck
and stomach.

The little blue heron starts its life
as a pure-white bird.
It turns to a deep blue
as it gets older.

It is easy to confuse it with
the snowy egret, which is
about the same size, except
the snowy egret has black
legs and yellow feet.

Here and on the next page are
little green herons. They have an
amazing ability to produce a long neck from
what seems like no visible neck at all.

They are quite distinct
from the other herons.

Besides the pelican, the great egret, or American egret, is one of the friendlier birds when it comes to humans. Most every neighborhood close to the water has one, affectionately named, that comes around daily for a handout. Some will eat out of your hand once they get to know you and even impatiently peck at a window for attention.

Originally from Southern Europe and Africa, the cattle egret was first seen in the United States in 1952. Now they are pretty much everywhere. Although they too resemble the snowy egret, cattle egrets have black feet. They are very adaptable— you may see them next to the road, in a freshwater ditch, saltwater bay; they can eat anything, anywhere. Cattle egrets are often seen around, what else, cattle. The cattle stir up insects while grazing, which makes finding the next meal an easy job for the egret.

The snowy egret, much smaller than the great egret, is a frequent visitor around fishing piers and also eager for any handout that may come its way. You can distinguish it from the other white birds because the snowy egret wears bright yellow "snowshoes." It also has a yellow stripe up the back of its black legs and its beak is a solid black.

Breeding plumage of the snowy egret is really quite spectacular. I can't begin to portray the elegance of it.

The beautiful white ibis is one of those energetic feeders as it probes the mud with its long orange bill.

Ibis generally feed together in groups, sometimes 10 or 15 miles away from where they roost. They eat crustaceans, fish, snails and other small delicacies. The brownish one on the bottom left is an immature white ibis.
The scarlet ibis on the right are native to South America.

The appropriately-named skimmer flies just above the waterline with its lower beak cutting through the surf in search of small unsuspecting fish. The specialized lower bill is longer than the upper one and gives the skimmer this strange appearance. They feed anytime but mostly at dusk, or even at night when the water is calmer and the fish are closer to the surface.

This little guy, the sandwich tern, can easily be identified by its yellow-tipped beak. Think of it as a spot of mustard on the bill. Terns are sometimes confused with gulls, but they are much smaller, their beaks sharper, and they have a forked tail.

Identifying birds can be very confusing because plumage on many birds changes dramatically between the summer and winter months. A Forster's tern, on the left above, and a common tern are in their winter plumage. In the summer the plumage on their heads becomes a cap of black.

The royal tern has this tuft of strange-looking feathers sticking out of its head. Like the skimmers, terns like to stay together in large groups on the beach. They can hover in the air for quite a long time, then quickly dive into the water when they spot a fish.

The American oystercatcher uses its long, orange wedgelike bill to drill into soft muddy areas to find oysters and clams. Before the oyster has a chance to close its shell, the beak has found its way in and severs the muscle.

Below is a beach I have visited often. Early in the morning seems to be a good time to see birds feeding. I always like the early morning quiet and the long blue shadows. There are so many shore birds to paint. The morning I was here, I found ibis taking advantage of the low tide.

There are many kinds of
sandpipers, too many to paint
for now, but here are two.
These are sanderlings. They
race about the beaches
on their short legs,
dodging waves
and people
at breakneck speed.

The amazing thing
about these little birds is that
they nest in the Arctic
and migrate to here
and as far south as Argentina.

The stilt likes lakes and fields
best, but is seen along the shore
as well. Their long legs
enable them to feed in waters
where it may be too deep
for other small
birds.

Although the wood stork brings to mind many childhood stories, it is anything but a romantic-looking creature.

The wood stork is the only stork that lives in the United States. It fishes by feel and not by sight. Its sensitive beak quickly snaps shut the instant it comes upon a passing fish.

Here an egret preens its feathers where its beak cannot reach them.
The next morning finds more sandpipers along the shore.

Here is a bird that has become a symbol of Florida, yet it is not even remotely part of Florida. The only place you will see them is at tourist attractions. If you see one in the wild it has probably escaped. Yet the state uses the flamingo in its advertising as if it were the only bird in Florida. I'll never understand why they do that.

The racetrack at Hialeah brought flamingos in from Cuba back in 1931. Because their wings were not clipped or pinioned, the flamingos flew away the next day. There were sightings around Florida for a while after that. In 1937 they tried again and this time fixed them so they couldn't fly. The birds, or rather their relatives, have been there ever since. They even nest and raise about 65 young each year. But flamingos mainly live on the islands and shores of the Caribbean where they get the diet they need to maintain their pink color.

The roseate spoonbill
is found in limited numbers
in Florida, Louisiana
and Texas.
To me, it is one of the
most beautiful
of our shore birds.

They feed by swinging
their partly opened bill
from side to side
through the muddy water.
When nerve endings
on their bills sense a
small fish, crustacean,
or insect, they quickly
snap their bills shut.

In 1939 only 30 of these beautiful creatures still existed in Florida. Their numbers have since increased considerably in Florida and Texas, and although they are protected from hunters, their habitat is vanishing at such a rate it's a wonder any wild birds remain. It would be a shame to lose wondrous things such as these in the name of beachfront condominiums and progress.

The sandhill crane prefers lakes
and fields to the shore, but
they are so large and distinctive
I thought I would include them.
Some of these cranes lose their
flight feathers during the
molting season and they
remain flightless
for a few weeks
until new ones
grow in.

From the side
like this
you can see
right through
the nostril
of its 6-inch
beak.

The frigate bird is sometimes called
the Man-o'-War. Weighing only
3 pounds or less, its wings extend
more than 7 feet. It is one of the
world's most superb flyers, capable
of soaring for hours and hours
on the wind.

notice the forked tail.

Although it can deftly catch food for itself by
swooping down on fish, the Man-o'-War has earned
its name by its bold and persistent harassment of other
birds who have already caught fish, forcing them to drop their catch,
which the Man-o'-War then retrieves in midair.

The osprey is sometimes mistaken for the bald eagle while in flight.

The osprey builds large nests. Although they like tall trees, I've seen them use telephone poles and even a TV antenna at someone's house for a nesting place.

Florida has more bald eagles than any other state, except Alaska.

This is a black vulture.

Vultures are not what you would call an
attractive bird, nor would you want
one for a pet. As scavengers, though,
they do help clean up what no one
else cares to touch.

When you think about it, there's
not much difference between
killing, then eating, dead animals
and finding one already
dead and eating it, as
the vulture does.

Turkey vultures have a red head.
Both kinds are pretty much
the same.

Quite beautiful when in the air.

The anhinga catches fish by diving.
They don't like to be around people very much,
and will usually fly away or plunge into the
water and disappear if you get
too close. With its head out of
water it resembles a snake,
hence the nickname
"snake bird."
Some call it a water turkey,
for what reason
I don't know.

Its sharp beak and long neck
help it spear fish.

Notice the big webbed feet for swimming.

The cormorant is sometimes mistaken for the anhinga.
They both dive for food and must perch after fishing to dry their wings.
They hold them to the sun and breeze for some time before flying again,
because unlike ducks their feathers are not waterproof. If they were,
they would not be able to submerge.

One difference between the cormorant and
the anhinga is the cormorant's hooked bill.
Cormorants generally dive from 5 to 25 feet
and stay under anywhere from 30 to 70
seconds, but some of these birds have
been caught in fishermen's nets
100 feet below the surface.

Here you can see the
cormorant's hooked bill.

The variety of life God created is amazing.
All those specialized abilities and features. Hooked bills,
sharp, pointed bills, feathers that shed water and
those that don't. Webbed feet for swimming,
long, thin legs for wading. All accomplish
a purpose for that particular animal.

The cormorant was once used in Asia to catch fish.
Cord leashes prevented it from swallowing its catch.
When the bird surfaced, the owner would
remove the fish from its throat.
It was allowed to swallow every fifth fish
or so. This kind of fishing is no longer
economical but is still done in Japan
for tourists.

Stilt houses like this are scattered throughout the South.
These at New Port Richey are about a mile offshore and were built
around the 1920s by mullet fishermen.

Now they are
primarily owned by
weekenders wanting a place
to get away from it all.

Lighthouses stand as monuments to seafarers, and have become an aesthetic symbol of our nautical heritage. Besides that, they are simply nice to look at. There is a beauty in functional simplicity that I have always enjoyed.

This is the lighthouse at Cape San Blas near the Florida Panhandle. There has been a light there since 1838.

In 1847, it blew down and another was built at a cost of $8,000. That light blew down four years later. A third lighthouse cost $12,000. Within a few months of its completion, it too was leveled by a storm. Did this stop them? Of course not. A fourth light was built just in time for the Civil War. And guess what? They burned it down, at least all that would burn. As if all this weren't enough, erosion crept in, undermining the light, and it fell over in 1882. A fifth lighthouse was erected in 1885 some 900 feet inland, but within nine years it was left standing in the surf, an offshore lighthouse. Not its purpose at all. So it was moved inland one final time... I think. Hindsight would indicate that removal of the shoal of which the light warned would have been a more practical solution...

but there is something about a lighthouse.

I tried to get permission to go to
the top of the light, but government
red tape sufficiently frustrated
me and I gave up. I went back
for one more look, and, lucky
me, these two coast guardsmen,
whose job it is to maintain
the light, happened by and
gave me the grand tour of
this and another lighthouse
as well.

A 232-step climb brought me to the top of this magnificent lighthouse near St. Augustine. The Fresnel lens is more than large enough to walk around in. Absolutely beautiful! I felt like a human flower inside a giant cut-glass vase atop a 150-foot pedestal. What an experience!

And it's much easier going down than it is walking up.

Back to the Gulf side not far from Apalachicola, St. Marks lighthouse stands like a jewel in the midst of a 65,000-acre wildlife refuge. I was there on a warm sunny day. Egrets and herons were everywhere, quietly fishing for their breakfast. I have never experienced such a peaceful place, the stillness and silence broken only by an occasional hum of a mullet boat motoring by. Thank goodness there are still places like this for us to enjoy.

Four feet thick at the base, this lighthouse built in 1829 supports a lens looking much like a sculptured glass pineapple.

This beautiful lighthouse graces the sands of Boca Grande.

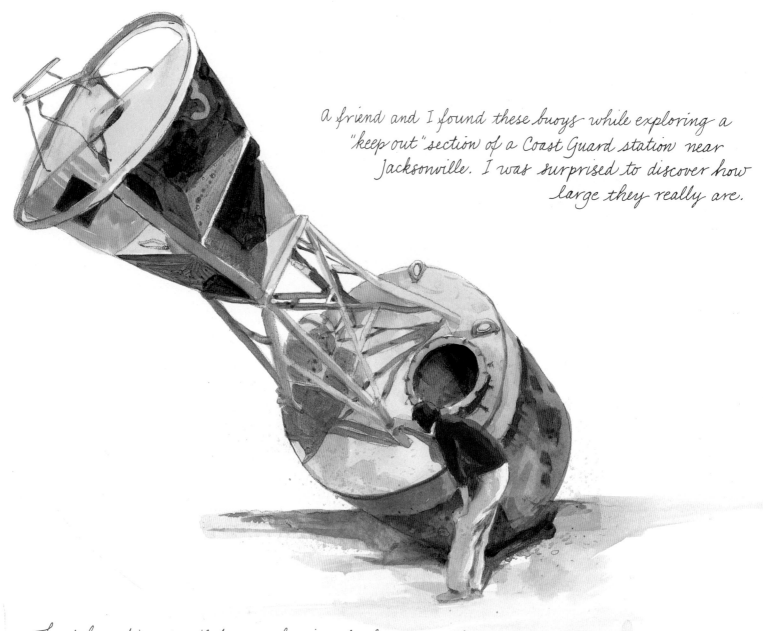

A friend and I found these buoys while exploring a "keep out" section of a Coast Guard station near Jacksonville. I was surprised to discover how large they really are.

The information stenciled onto the side of this one I thought was really funny. It said, "approximate weight 11,382 lbs." I wondered if the exact weight might be 11,382 pounds and 4 ounces.

I'm not the type of person who would care to live on a boat and I don't even know much about the mechanics of it all. I do, however, like to sail, watch the water and weather, and eat sandwiches while lying on a soft cushion on deck.

And this is the boat I have done the most of that on. It belongs to a good friend of mine. Bob Hite, whose boat this is, would like me to tell you that it's a ketch of the Crocker design built in 1958, is 42 feet, 9 inches, has a beam of 12 feet, 2 inches, is 36 feet at the waterline, has a 6-foot draft, has 8,000 lbs. of external lead ballast, and 880 square feet of working sail. I, on the other hand, want to know what kind of sandwiches we will have on board.

I do find it a beautiful boat and have done many paintings of it, not to mention the many wonderful hours of conversation and friendship that always accompanies a good sail aboard "The Kinship".

Boats fit into two categories, those which need to be worked on and those which need to be worked on right away. I think boats require more attention than anything I know. It's times like this when it's nice to have a friend who owns the boat. Boats are generally hauled out once a year, giving artists like me a great opportunity to do paintings of them on the ways. I'll never understand, though, why these boats don't always fall over. The jackstands holding them up never have looked sufficient.

To me, a boat like this is more like a sculpture than anything else - especially when its out of the water.

This marina sits in front of
my favorite restaurant,
Jesse's Dockside in Dunedin, Florida.

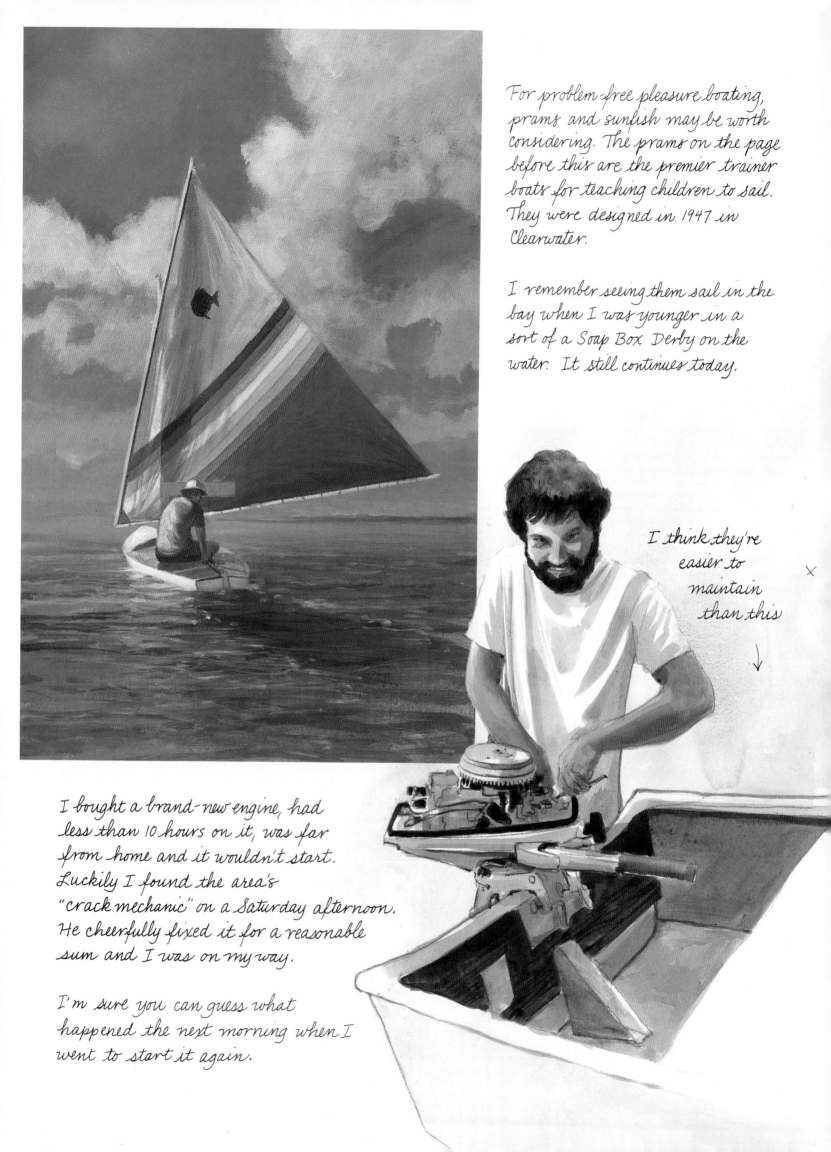

For problem-free pleasure boating, prams and sunfish may be worth considering. The prams on the page before this are the premier trainer boats for teaching children to sail. They were designed in 1947 in Clearwater.

I remember seeing them sail in the bay when I was younger in a sort of a Soap Box Derby on the water. It still continues today.

I think they're easier to maintain than this

I bought a brand-new engine, had less than 10 hours on it, was far from home and it wouldn't start. Luckily I found the area's "crack mechanic" on a Saturday afternoon. He cheerfully fixed it for a reasonable sum and I was on my way.

I'm sure you can guess what happened the next morning when I went to start it again.

With these little boats
it's easy to get right up to
shallow places like this.

Usually not much attention is paid to the dinghy, but I find some of them to be quite worthy of painting.

I call this real serious fishing. That includes not only the fishermen but also the boat and the equipment that goes along with it.

I'm sure it must be a thrill to bring in a catch like this.

A few years from now, this same fish will most likely grow to proportions like this when the story is told.

This is not a sport for the passive fisherman.
Buckling yourself into one of these
fighting chairs for hours at a time,
trying to land a 450 pound marlin, seems
more like torture than fun. In fact,
the chair itself reminds me of the electric chair
or at best something from a 1920s dentist office.

Of course, you don't need a $750,000 Hatteras
Sport Fisherman and a $12,000 fighting
chair to catch fish and, frankly, sitting
on an old 5-gallon bucket looks
just as pleasant, maybe more so.

I think I'll title this painting "Patience".

Fishing gives people the chance to sit and be non-productive and not feel guilty about it. That has a lot of merit I believe, and I keep telling myself I'll try it someday. It looks real nice.

My girl, Lauren, sits down beside a fisherman and starts a conversation.
What could be nicer on a warm sunny day? Just watching
the clouds move across the sky and the reflection of it
all mirrored in the water is reward enough, even
when the fish aren't biting.

A walk on the beach isn't a bad idea either. And you can
always find some little treasure if it's a beach like this one below.
It may be a little shell or a gnarly piece of driftwood
that looks like a bird's head.

Or just another chance to watch pelicans fly.

Sandburs are always laying in wait
for an unsuspecting bare foot to come along.
Before you pull one out of your paining foot,
moisten the tips of your fingers with your tongue;
then it won't stick to your fingers.

Here's one of those small treasures that brings wonderment to the eyes of a beautiful little girl. A sharing experience like this is a treasure for everyone and a moment that makes all else seem insignificant.

A deserted beach makes a perfect spot for some quiet reflection. The Australian pine offers an umbrella of lacy pine needles that carpets the ground below it.

The Australian pine is my all-time favorite tree, but many others don't share my feelings. Here's why. The root system is shallow so it can blow over easily; nothing else will grow beneath it, so it tends to push out other vegetation, and it is very aggressive. Once it gets going it is hard to get rid of. I don't find these reasons much of a problem, yet some places won't even allow them to be planted.

To see a mass of these trees with their rich green cover above and a thick bed of brown pine needles below is like something out of a fantasyland. Beautiful!

Of course, no tree symbolizes
Southern shores like the palm.
Thousands of species exist
in the world, and I
could fill a book on just
palms of the South.
Here are just a few.

← Coconut palm
The coconut is not really a
nut at all, but a seed,
one of the largest seeds in the world.

Cabbage palm
This is the state tree of
Florida. The thatched pattern
on the trunk, called boots, is what
remains from the base of old leaves.
↓

Sometimes they fall off leaving a bare trunk,
and sometimes they don't, making the
same trees look quite different.
The heart of this palm can be eaten
in salads, but then the tree will die.

The Washingtonian
Palm

This is a palm you see lining many roads
and causeways in the South. I've seen them
grow to 80 feet and higher. If the old leaves
aren't trimmed off the trunk, they will remain
on there for years and years.

Another graceful coconut palm in the warm summer breeze at Bahia Honda State Park in the Keys.

I wish people would leave
palmettos alone. Every time
I see a lot being developed,
they are the first things
to go. They are a beautiful
plant, always green, and
require no care.
They are part of the
Southern landscape
that is totally
ignored.
I hope someday it will
become fashionable to leave what
already grows naturally. My yard
is full of them, hundreds in fact, and
I enjoy them immensely.

The royal palm is very distinctive
because of its smooth, bright-green trunk
right below the leaves.
It is the most stately
of the palms and because
they freeze easily, they can be
found only in the
Southern part of Florida
from Sarasota on down.

This palm is a favorite with homeowners – at least in Clearwater where I live. It grows a heavy sheath with small yellow flowers in it. Later, hundreds of bright orange seeds about the size of chestnuts appear.

When I was a boy, I would use them as convenient ammunition to launch at neighbor's mailboxes while riding my bike.

Cocos Plumosa →

← Date Palm

Here is a strangler fig doing what it does best. An unfortunate cabbage palm is the victim of this most unusual plant. The strangler fig started its career as a seed at the top of a tree, probably dropped there by a passing bird. It sends aerial roots down the trunk. When they take hold in the ground, the fig then sends new branches upward. By starting at the top of the tree, it has an advantage over trees which start at the ground, because it gets better light.

The host eventually dies because its trunk can't expand, or because the fig covers the tree with so much shade it can't thrive. At any rate, this takes decades to do. I've seen these mostly down toward Captiva or in the Everglades.

This little painting was done at Cedar Key on a cold morning right at sunrise. I like the way the long shadows cast themselves on the ground, allowing those thin slivers of warm morning light to shine through. And again, more cabbage palms.

I have flown a hot-air balloon for many years. Every time I fly, it is a special experience.

It has given me a view of the world few people share. It gives me an appreciation of the winds and the weather and the world below. It gives me a sense of how fragile and frail things are, including me.

With the exception of a few tourist shops, Cedar Key is
one of those fishing villages that hasn't changed a whole lot over the years.
This stilt house is one of those things every artist who goes there paints
at one time or another.

Diving for sponges in a suit like this is pretty much a thing of the past even in the Greek community of Tarpon Springs. Wet suits are used today, and considering that a rubberized canvas suit like this weighs a total of 172 pounds, it's a wonder they're still in use at all.

The helmet alone weighs 38 pounds and the leaded shoes each weigh 12 pounds.

This boat takes 30 people out at a time and motors a short way down the Anclote River where six or eight times a day this diver dons his suit. He jumps overboard and a few minutes later – to the delight of everyone on board – comes to the surface with a sponge in his hand. The St. Nicholas Boat Lines have been doing these exhibition dives since 1924.

Commercial harvesting is done year-round at Tarpon Springs and to this day the sponge industry is still a major part of this interesting town.

Grass sponge   Wool sponge   Finger sponge   Yellow sponge

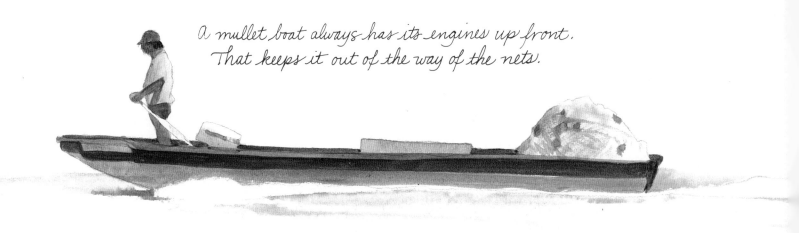

A mullet boat always has its engines up front.
That keeps it out of the way of the nets.

I'll never understand why these nets don't get hopelessly tangled every time they're used. I have trouble keeping a 20-foot extension cord straight.

The nets are dropped off as the mullet are circled. A real good strike could bring in 4,000 pounds of mullet.

Mullet nets are made of monofilament line. The fish try to swim through it and get caught by their gills. To catch large mullet, a 4-inch net is used, allowing small fish to swim through. A smaller 2½-inch net snags the smaller fish, and the larger fish bounce off.

A mullet boat carries 400 to 600 yards of net, although only 200 yards may be let out. All this net is weighted with lead. Not an easy job hauling all this stuff. To remove the mullet, called shucking, it is pulled head first through the net.

Shrimping is a big industry in the South and requires quite a bit of equipment. I wandered through a warehouse near Jacksonville and found this interesting array of blocks used on shrimp boats.

Shrimp boats come in all sizes. A boat like this might travel hundreds of miles to work. The nets are attached to "doors". When pulled through the water, the doors act like wings and spread up to 200 feet of net across the bottom. A chain that goes across the mouth of the net helps stir up the shrimp and into the net they go. A net lasts from 6 months to a year - or maybe only 2 minutes if they tangle with rocks, anchors and such.

Although part of a shrimp net, or trawl, is machine-made, they are finished off, and of course repaired, by hand. I came across a shop in Fernandina Beach, just north of Jacksonville, which has specialized in net-making for three generations. The owner, William, was unbelievably fast at sewing these nets together.

Working boats have a character that pleasure boats seem to lack.
After painting these, I began to think of how they sort of look like human faces,
each having similarities, yet each having definite unique features.

This got me to wondering
if there might be any similarities
between the boats
and the men who work them.

Both the boats and the faces
are well-seasoned by wind
and weathered by years of
experience.

These are a few of the men
who sat for me in my studio.
While I drew them, they
shared their stories with me—

stories as
interesting as
their faces.

What
character.

In their eyes you can almost read the experiences it took a lifetime to acquire. You can see this warmth right through the rough exterior.

Grouper Boat — This bottom-long-line reel can put out as much as 20 miles of fishing line and hooks. Bandit reels drop one line to the bottom. They also have many hooks.

Bandit reels

Bottom line reel

These wooden traps are for stone crabs. With repairs, they last about three years. This man has 1,500 of them.

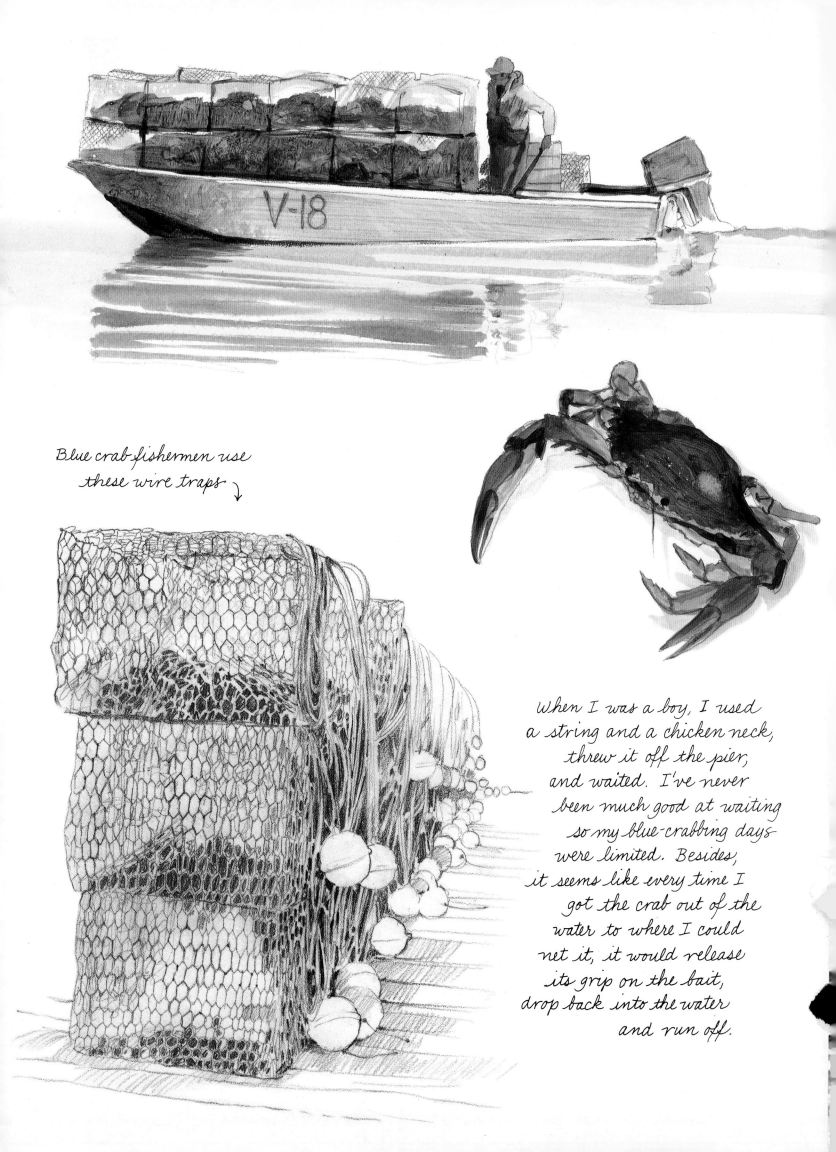

Blue crab fishermen use
these wire traps ↓

When I was a boy, I used
a string and a chicken neck,
threw it off the pier,
and waited. I've never
been much good at waiting
so my blue-crabbing days
were limited. Besides,
it seems like every time I
got the crab out of the
water to where I could
net it, it would release
its grip on the bait,
drop back into the water
and run off.

Shrimp boats ↗

This is a long-liner. It drops off these floats called highfliers with lines and hooks extending from pole to pole. They catch swordfish, shark, grouper and snapper.

Oysters are one seafood I have never acquired a taste for. The idea of putting raw oysters in my mouth is not my idea of a pleasant experience. A lot of oysters come from the Apalachicola area. They lay just under the mud on the bottom of the bays and are dug out with a double rake scissored near the end. Here at Eastpoint, oysters are shucked and the shells are discarded outside through a chute in the wall.

This lady told me she had been doing this since she was 15.

There is such a richness in texture and character along the Southern shores that it is impossible to touch on it all. I have only put my brush to subjects that happen to interest me at the moment, those things that caught my eye.

Some areas seemed a bit devoid of interesting images, especially where condominiums took their share of the beaches, but even then, a thorny sandbur plant with its runners gripping the shifting sand provided a nice bit of nature to focus on.

I guess it's how we look at things that determines their beauty and worth. There were obvious subjects I wanted to paint but didn't get around to. This was by no means a definitive look at Southern shores. It was a learning experience for me and it is just a taste of what is there. The more I painted the more I felt there was to do and the more I did, the more I felt I had left undone. Much of it will still be here for the generations to come and much of it will be gone. Things are changing so quickly, some for the better and some for the worse.

My feeling is that we need to leave as much of it alone as we can; to destroy as little as possible, to live and work with what nature has given us. If we can do that and still be comfortable, our world will be better because of it.

If only we could take more time to look at what is here for us to see. Beauty is all around us. I have seen it in the discarded hulls of forgotten boats and in crumbling piers. Beauty comes in large and small packages— in towering, 40,000-foot cumulus clouds building up over the open sea and in delicate and fragile wildflowers growing unexpectedly between cracked concrete in a sea wall.

And if we take the time to really see what is here, surely we will come to love and understand the land, the water, and everything it supports. My wish is that the focus on growth is not at the expense of what it took nature thousands of years to create.

RLBansemer

Mobile

Pensacola

Panama
Ca

New
Orleans